A Note From Denise Renner

The Word of God is so powerful in our lives. It is essential that every person spend time with God and study His Word in order to stay spiritually strong in these last days.

This study guide corresponds to my *TIME With Denise Renner* TV program by the same title that can be viewed at **deniserenner.org**. My desire is that through these lessons, you find the encouragement and freedom in Christ that you need. I believe the Holy Spirit is going to speak to you through the words you read in this study tool and that as you begin to use it, you will be *propelled* into the abundant life God has planned for you. I encourage you to make the effort to receive all He has for you and all He wants to do in you — it will definitely be worth it!

Whether you have walked with the Lord a long time or have just begun to follow Him, there is so much He wants to give you from His Word. He sees where you are, and He wants to meet you there.

> **Therefore do not worry about tomorrow, for tomorrow will worry about its own things. Sufficient for the day is its own trouble.**
> **— Matthew 6:34**

Your sister and friend in Jesus Christ,

Denise Renner

Denise Renner

How Heaven Answers When We Worship

Copyright © 2025 by Denise Renner
1814 W. Tacoma St.
Broken Arrow, Oklahoma 74012-1406

Published by Rick Renner Ministries
www.renner.org

ISBN 13: 978-1-6675-1140-5

ISBN 13 eBook: 978-1-6675-1141-2

TOPIC

The Answer to Your Problem Is Found in Worship

SCRIPTURES

1. **Genesis 8:20-22** — Then Noah built an altar to the Lord, and took of every clean animal and of every clean bird, and offered burnt offerings on the altar. And the Lord smelled a soothing aroma. Then the Lord said in His heart, "I will never again curse the ground for man's sake, although the imagination of man's heart is evil from his youth; nor will I again destroy every living thing as I have done. "While the earth remains, seedtime and harvest, cold and heat, winter and summer, and day and night shall not cease."

2. **Romans 12:1** — I beseech you therefore, brethren, by the mercies of God, that you present your bodies a living sacrifice, holy, acceptable to God, which is your reasonable service.

3. **Genesis 9:1-3** — So God blessed Noah and his sons, and said to them: "Be fruitful and multiply, and fill the earth. And the fear of you and the dread of you shall be on every beast of the earth, on every bird of the air, on all that move on the earth, and on all the fish of the sea. They are given into your hand. Every moving thing that lives shall be food for you. I have given you all things, even as the green herbs."

4. **Genesis 9:7** — And as for you, be fruitful and multiply; bring forth abundantly in the earth and multiply in it.

5. **Genesis 9:16** — The rainbow shall be in the cloud, and I will look on it to remember the everlasting covenant between God and every living creature of all flesh that is on the earth.

6. **2 Corinthians 2:15** — For we are to God the fragrance of Christ among those who are being saved and among those who are perishing.

7. **Ephesians 5:2** — And walk in love, as Christ also has loved us and given Himself for us, an offering and a sacrifice to God for a sweet-smelling aroma.

SYNOPSIS

The five lessons in this study on *How Heaven Answers When We Worship* will focus on the following topics:

- The Answer to Your Problem Is Found in Worship
- In Worship the Battle Is Not Yours
- You Are Strengthened Through Worship
- Worship Can Shake Things Up
- Ultimate Worship

The emphasis of this lesson:

Answers from Heaven await us when we worship God! From the days of the Flood when Noah first made his sacrifice after the ark came to rest safely until this very moment, God has kept His promises — and He continues to do so. Those promised blessings and the answers to all our needs come to us through worship.

When we worship God, His peace floods our heart and mind. Miraculous things happen as we make time to praise God. We receive answers from Heaven!

God Receives Our Worship

Historians say there's a particular place in Turkey where Noah built his altar to sacrifice unto the Lord after they exited the ark. Denise visited the site in person and said:

> When I saw this rock and where it had been chiseled so that the blood of the sacrifices could flow down, I started weeping because this was the first place of sacrifices unto the Lord. After everything had been destroyed by the Flood, Noah's altar was the very first place where worship took place and sacrifices were given unto the Lord. It made me consider how powerful it is when we worship Him.

When we truly worship God and open up by surrendering places within our heart to Him, He begins to speak to us. He gives us answers. He tells us that He loves us. There's nothing like worship! In fact, Jesus said that the Father *seeks* such to worship Him (*see* John 4:23). The Bible says that

His eyes go to and fro across the earth to find those who will worship Him (*see* 2 Chronicles 16:9). In Genesis 8:20-22, God's Word says:

> **Then Noah built an altar to the Lord, and took of every clean animal and of every clean bird, and offered burnt offerings on the altar. And the Lord smelled a soothing aroma. Then the Lord said in His heart, 'I will never again curse the ground for man's sake, although the imagination of man's heart is evil from his youth; nor will I again destroy every living thing as I have done. While the earth remains seedtime and harvest, cold and heat, winter and summer, and day and night shall not cease.'**

When Noah made that sacrifice, worshiped, and surrendered unto the Lord from that place, God began speaking. He received Noah's sacrifice. That's the first thing that happens when we open our heart and worship the Lord. He *receives* our worship! He accepts our heart as a sacrifice unto Him.

God Speaks When We Worship

Romans 12:1 says, "I beseech you therefore, brethren, by the mercies of God, that you present your bodies a living sacrifice, holy, acceptable to God, which is your reasonable service." God is interested in our coming before Him. He desires that we give as much as we can out of our heart as we worship and speak to Him, surrendering to Him.

In that place of worship and surrender, God speaks. That's exactly what happened with Noah. God spoke and said, "I'll never curse the earth again." In Genesis 8:20, He declared, "While the earth remains seedtime and harvest, cold and heat, winter and summer, and day and night shall not cease."

It has been thousands of years since He said that, and for thousands of years, He has kept His promise. The Bible says in Hebrews 13:8, "Jesus Christ is the same yesterday, today, and forever." God kept His promise *then*, and God keeps His promise *now*. His promises are yes and amen (*see* 2 Corinthians 1:20).

God Opens Up Answers When We Worship

Let's take a look at what happened after Noah worshiped God on the first alter after the Flood:

> So God blessed Noah and his sons, and said to them: 'Be fruitful and multiply, and fill the earth. And the fear of you and the dread of you shall be on every beast of the earth, on every bird of the air, on all that move on the earth, and on all the fish of the sea. They are given into your hand. Every moving thing that lives shall be food for you. I have given you all things, even as the green herbs.'
>
> — Genesis 9:1-3

God was essentially saying to Noah, "You do not have to fear the lion. You don't have to fear the bear, the tiger, or the snake. You don't have to fear any of these animals because you now have the power to rule over them."

This is awesome because when the animals got off the ark, the lions were still lions; the bears were still bears. And even though the lions and bears would become hungry and soon begin looking for prey, God protected Noah and his family from all the danger of those predatory animals.

God also made provision for Noah and his family. The Lord basically said to them, "You can eat any living thing you want to eat.' God opened up protection and provision for Noah and his family after they worshiped Him. Likewise, as we worship Him, God opens to us the answers to our every need.

Be Fruitful and Multiply!

When God brings answers, He often also brings instructions. In Genesis 9:7, we read the instructions God gave to Noah and his family: "And as for you, be fruitful and multiply; bring forth abundantly in the earth and multiply in it." Denise shared her insights into this verse:

> I've read that verse for years, and I always thought 'be fruitful and multiply' meant: 'Keep replenishing the earth by having children.' But as I was studying it, I saw something else. I saw a command to us all in the words: 'Be fruitful and multiply.' What has God has given us? What talents and gifts do we have? What kind of mind do we have? Let's 'be fruitful and multiply' and make more of what we have!

If you have a talent, make more of it. If you are a manager, study how to become a better one. If you have money, study how to make more and give it away. Be fruitful and then multiply. Give out of what you have to help somebody else. When you give what you have, it doesn't stay as is. It multiplies! So multiply what you have.

Do you remember when Jesus was talking about the talents (*see* Matthew 25:14-30)? He said the man gave one of his servants five talents, he gave another servant two, and he gave a third servant one talent. The one with five talents multiplied his from five to ten. The one with two multiplied his from two to four. But Jesus said the man with one talent was a wicked servant because he was afraid.

It is not God's will for us to hold on to what He has given us. His will is for us to multiply it. God was not simply saying to Noah, "Have babies and replenish the earth with more people." He was saying, "What you have, Noah — what you and your family can do with your hands and your minds — be fruitful and multiply and *use* it."

Make the Most of What He Has Given You

There was once a world-renowned violinist who had quit performing. He was 75-80 years old, and he was still regularly practicing playing the violin. Someone asked him, "Why are you still practicing?" The violinist said, "So that I will get better." This man was being fruitful and multiplying. Nobody was listening to him play live anymore, yet he continued to steward the gift he had been given and multiply it.

Denise shared a story of one woman of God, who said she didn't feel like she had any talent. The woman said, "God, You didn't give me any talent. I'm talentless. What am I going to do?" God said to that woman, "Do you have hands? Do you have feet? Do you have a mouth? Use what you have. Use your smile. Give your smile away to somebody. Give your kindness away to somebody. When you give it away, you multiply it." This is a powerful revelation that came as a result of worship.

Imagine what God might say to you if you spend time worshiping Him. Open up the book of Psalms and read them aloud to Him. Tell the Lord how magnificent, how great, and how wonderful He is. Let Him know how thankful you are to Him and see what that time of worship opens up to you. Worship is so powerful!

We Have an Everlasting Covenant With Him

In Genesis 9, God promised that He would not destroy the earth again with water. Can you imagine the first time Noah and his family saw rain after the Flood? If God hadn't made that promise they would have been scared that the world would be flooded again. And what about the animals? When water started falling out of the sky, they would have been scared.

But God offered a comforting word. He said, "I will never destroy the world like this again by water. I'm going to give you a sign of My promise." Then He placed the rainbow in the sky, and we see that sign even to this day as a reminder of what He said.

Genesis 9:16 says, "The rainbow shall be in the cloud, and I will look on it to remember the everlasting covenant between God and every living creature of all flesh that is on the earth." This verse tells us that God spoke the rainbow into existence as a sign of His trustworthiness. God said He would look at that rainbow and remember the promise He made.

We Carry the Fragrance of Christ

Genesis 8:20 says that when Noah made his sacrifice, it was a "soothing aroma" unto the Lord. When we worship, we offer a sweet, soothing aroma unto the Lord. In Second Corinthians 2:15, we read, "For we are to God the fragrance of Christ among those who are being saved and among those who are perishing."

You may not think of yourself as special. Or you may simply be having a hard day. But know this: You are giving off an aroma. According to Second Corinthians 2:15, you are the fragrance of Christ. Just like Noah's sacrifice was a soothing aroma unto the Lord, *you* are a soothing aroma to the Lord — because Jesus lives within you.

Ephesians 5:2 declares, "And walk in love, as Christ also has loved us and given Himself for us, an offering and a sacrifice to God for a sweet-smelling aroma." When Jesus died for us, His sacrifice was a sweet-smelling aroma to God. Why? Because God knew that He was going to receive us. He knew He was going to live in us and that we would bring a fragrance unto Him because Christ lives in us.

Quiet Yourself and Worship Him

Worship is so powerful; it doesn't have to be hard. We can simply open up the Psalms and read the words of praise and worship to the Lord. We can declare, "Lord, I'm going to be quiet before You. I'm not going to answer the phone. I'm not going to look at the computer or the television. I'm going to quiet myself right now and worship You. I recognize that I am a sweet-smelling aroma unto You as Christ was to You when He died."

He loves us so much! Worship opens up Heaven to give answers to us. And when we worship Him, we are a sweet-smelling fragrance unto Him!

STUDY QUESTIONS

**Be diligent to present yourself approved to God, a worker
who does not need to be ashamed, rightly dividing the word of truth.**
— 2 Timothy 2:15

1. John 4:23 and 24 says, "But the hour is coming, and now is, when the true worshipers will worship the Father in spirit and truth; for the Father is seeking such to worship Him. God is Spirit, and those who worship Him must worship in spirit and truth." According to this passage, what is the Father seeking?
2. Read Matthew 25:14-30. How can you apply this parable to your life? According to this lesson, what are some ways a person can "be fruitful and multiply"?

PRACTICAL APPLICATION

**But be doers of the word,
and not hearers only, deceiving yourselves.**
—James 1:22

1. Take an objective look at yourself. What has God graced you with that you can give to others? Are you a singer? Maybe it's time to join the church choir. Do you love people? How about becoming a greeter to welcome others into the house of God? Are you gifted with a servant's heart? Perhaps you would make an outstanding usher. Are you called to preach the Word? Then take the opportunity before you, no matter how small it may seem — and preach! Come before the Lord with a humble heart and commit to giving out what He entrusted to

you. And don't delay or hold back! Take a moment to pray a prayer of consecration to the Lord and commit to using your talent for Him.

2. Denise spoke of quieting ourselves before the Lord as we come into His presence. This may mean we silence our phone, get away from our other devices, and focus solely on Him. Psalm 131:2 says, "Surely I have calmed and quieted my soul...." What things typically serve as a distraction to you? What steps will you take to ensure they no longer take away from your time with the Lord?

3. When was the last time you pressed in and worshipped God while you were alone? Take time today to do that. Put on your favorite worship music and sing without restraint to the Lord or sing a new song to the Lord by letting it come right up out of your heart. Engage your heart as you worship Him. Be sincere and give Him your very best. If He speaks something to your heart or leads you to a verse of Scripture, esteem those things by writing them down and meditating on them. It's in His presence that answers come.

LESSON 2

TOPIC

In Worship the Battle Is Not Yours

SCRIPTURES

1. **2 Chronicles 20:3** — And Jehoshaphat feared, and set himself to seek the Lord, and proclaimed a fast throughout all Judah.

2. **2 Chronicles 20:6,7** — ...O Lord God of our fathers, are You not God in heaven, and do You not rule over all the kingdoms of the nations, and in Your hand is there not power and might, so that no one is able to withstand You? Are You not our God, who drove out the inhabitants of this land before Your people Israel, and gave it to the descendants of Abraham Your friend forever?

3. **2 Chronicles 20:11,12** — Here they are, rewarding us by coming to throw us out of Your possession which You have given us to inherit. O our God, will You not judge them? For we have no power against this great multitude that is coming against us; nor do we know what to do, but our eyes are upon You.

4. **2 Chronicles 20:15-22** — And he said, "Listen, all you of Judah and you inhabitants of Jerusalem, and you, King Jehoshaphat! Thus says the Lord to you: 'Do not be afraid nor dismayed because of this great multitude, for the battle is not yours, but God's. Tomorrow go down against them. They will surely come up by the Ascent of Ziz, and you will find them at the end of the brook before the Wilderness of Jeruel. You will not need to fight in this battle. Position yourselves, stand still and see the salvation of the Lord, who is with you, O Judah and Jerusalem!' Do not fear or be dismayed; tomorrow go out against them, for the Lord is with you." And Jehoshaphat bowed his head with his face to the ground, and all Judah and the inhabitants of Jerusalem bowed before the Lord, worshiping the Lord. Then the Levites of the children of the Kohathites and of the children of the Korahites stood up to praise the Lord God of Israel with voices loud and high. So they rose early in the morning and went out into the Wilderness of Tekoa; and as they went out, Jehoshaphat stood and said, "Hear me, O Judah and you inhabitants of Jerusalem: Believe in the Lord your God, and you shall be established; believe His prophets, and you shall prosper." And when he had consulted with the people, he appointed those who should sing to the Lord, and who should praise the beauty of holiness, as they went out before the army and were saying: "Praise the Lord, for His mercy endures forever." Now when they began to sing and to praise, the Lord set ambushes against the people of Ammon, Moab, and Mount Seir, who had come against Judah; and they were defeated.

5. **1 Peter 5:7** — Casting all your care upon Him, for He cares for you.

SYNOPSIS

When we face fearful moments in life, worship allows us to tap into God's mighty delivering power. We see this power in action in Second Chronicles. As King Jehoshaphat and the people of Judah faced an army three times their size, the Lord instructed them to worship Him. As they marched in faith and worshiped, God defeated Judah's enemy — and they reaped the spoils. We can do the same as we worship the Lord in faith!

The emphasis of this lesson:

Through worship, God comes into the situations we face with all His power to bring deliverance from the enemy. As we worship Him, the

circumstances we're in grow dim, His presence is magnified, and God goes before us to open up our path to victory.

Set Yourself To Seek the Lord

Often when problems come, we try to fix them ourselves. But the Word of God says that the battle is not ours. That's a powerful truth! In Second Chronicles 20, the people of Judah faced an enemy three times bigger than they were. To them, this enemy attack meant that every one of them would die. There seemed to be no way to defeat their foe, and they were sorely outnumbered.

Second Chronicles 20:3 says, "And Jehoshaphat feared, and set himself to seek the Lord, and proclaimed a fast throughout all Judah." Jehoshaphat was the king of Judah who was facing this threat against himself and his whole kingdom. The Scriptures say that he was afraid of the enemy army. So he "set himself to seek the Lord."

Likewise, when we get news that is threatening, we must refuse fear and choose to worship the Lord. We must set ourselves to seek the Lord, even when the pressures all around us may be screaming for us to move into doubt and worry. Denise shared the testimony of a friend of hers who faced a terrifying situation and decided to seek God.

This woman found her daughter unconscious one morning and took her to the hospital where she was admitted. There she learned her daughter had a horrible disease that had taken the lives of other children just that weekend.

Fear crowded in on this woman, saying, "Your daughter is going to die. What will you do if your daughter dies?" She was experiencing every emotion that fear can communicate. But she set herself to seek the Lord, and He said, "Don't fear."

The woman received that encouraging word from the Lord and laid hands on her daughter in faith, believing what He had said. God raised up the daughter — and there was no longer anything wrong with her. While others had perished from this disease, the little girl miraculously survived because her mother sought the Lord. This woman's testimony is a beautiful reminder of how we must refuse to be moved by our circumstances.

Remind Yourself of Who God Is

Jehoshaphat set himself to seek the Lord and proclaimed a fast. In Second Chronicles 20:6, we see that he spoke to all the people of Judah and prayed in their presence, "...O Lord God of our fathers, are You not God in heaven, and do You not rule over all the kingdoms of the nations, and in Your hand is there not power and might, so that no one is able to withstand You?" The king took leadership, and he told God who He is. Jehoshaphat was not doing this because God didn't know who He is. Rather, the king was reminding *himself* and his people who God is.

This is part of worship sometimes. People may come into the church when it's supposed to be a time of worship, yet they are occupied on their cell phones, or they talk in the middle of worship. But worship is a time to set ourselves to seek the Lord. We are to put distractions aside and rehearse who God is.

In this time of worship, open your heart and tell Him how wonderful He is. Declare that nothing is impossible for Him. That's what King Jehoshaphat was doing. He was saying to himself, to the people of Judah, and to God, "This situation is bad, but nothing is impossible for God!"

When difficult circumstances come into your life, you can do the same. Worship the Lord and say, "Lord, this may be bad, but You are greater! The Greater One is on the inside of me, and He's greater than he that's in this world. So I'm going to trust You, Lord."

In Second Chronicles 20:7, King Jehoshaphat went on to declare, "Are You not our God, who drove out the inhabitants of this land before Your people Israel, and gave it to the descendants of Abraham Your friend forever?" It's important that we remember who He is so that we are not overcome by the situation we are facing.

We are to remember that the name of Jesus is higher than any other name that is named. Cancer, relational problems, lung conditions, kidney issues, skin diseases — all these are names. But His name is above every other name. In worship, we can say, "God, this is bad, but Your name is higher."

The doctor may have given you bad news of a serious diagnosis. You can say, "Jesus, Your name is higher than that name. Your name is higher than cancer. Your name is higher than kidney disease. Your name is higher than heart failure." Like Jehoshaphat did, you can magnify God and proclaim the name of Jesus to be above every other name.

Make Your Petition in Faith

After he magnified the Lord, King Jehoshaphat told God the problem he was facing. In Second Chronicles 20:11 and 12, he said, "Here they are, rewarding us by coming to throw us out of Your possession which You have given us to inherit. O our God, will You not judge them? For we have no power against this great multitude that is coming against us; nor do we know what to do, but our eyes are upon You."

After Jehoshaphat's petition was made, God spoke through one of His prophets. You may not hear a prophet speak in answer to your prayers, but you can always hear the Holy Spirit speak in your heart. Denise shared that she found herself in a similar situation:

> I was facing a very difficult situation that didn't seem like it was turning around. I set aside one day to seek the Lord and fast, and I heard the Lord speak. It wasn't a prophet who came into the house and prophesied to me. It was the Holy Spirit on the inside who spoke to me. He said, "Denise, I've got this." All I needed was to know that He was on the case.

Your God is not far from you. He's right there on the inside of you. He cares for you, and He wants to give you the answer. In Second Chronicles 20:15, the prophet said, "…Listen, all you of Judah and you inhabitants of Jerusalem, and you, King Jehoshaphat! Thus says the Lord to you: 'Do not be afraid nor dismayed because of this great multitude, for the battle is not yours, but God's.'"

Cast Your Cares Upon Him

That battle you're facing is not yours! First Peter 5:7 says, "Casting all your care upon Him, for He cares for you." It's the same for you today as it was for King Jehoshaphat. God is saying to you, "That's not your battle. That's not your worry. Cast that care over on Me. You don't have to fight that battle. I've already fought it for you."

God essentially said the same thing to Jehoshaphat. The Lord already knew where the enemy army was, so he told Jehoshaphat and the people of Judah where to go. And then the prophet of the Lord went on to explain what the people were to do. Second Chronicles 20:17 says,

> **You will not need to fight in this battle. Position yourselves, stand still and see the salvation of the Lord, who is with you, O Judah and Jerusalem!' Do not fear or be dismayed; tomorrow go out against them, for the Lord is with you.**

God is not withholding answers from us. He wants to give us the answers we need for every situation. But many times, found within the answers He gives, is a set of instructions. We must do more than listen for His voice; we must also do what He says.

Worship Aligns Us With God's Power To Deliver Us

Second Chronicles 20:18 says, "And Jehoshaphat bowed his head with his face to the ground, and all Judah and the inhabitants of Jerusalem bowed before the Lord, worshiping the Lord." When they worshipped the Lord, they began to trust the Lord. They began to say, "We should not fear. We should not be dismayed. Let's do what He told us to do. Let's stand still and see the salvation of the Lord. Let's *believe*. The battle is not ours, but His."

When we worship the Lord, we align ourselves with Him and open Heaven, which allows His answers and His power to come into our lives. This is what the people of Judah did. They worshiped the Lord, and they lifted their voices. Second Chronicles 20:20 and 21 says:

> **So they rose early in the morning and went out into the Wilderness of Tekoa; and as they went out, Jehoshaphat stood and said, 'Hear me, O Judah and you inhabitants of Jerusalem: Believe in the Lord your God, and you shall be established; believe His prophets, and you shall prosper.' And when he had consulted with the people, he appointed those who should sing to the Lord, and who should praise the beauty of holiness, as they went out before the army and were saying: 'Praise the Lord, for His mercy *endures* forever.'**

They went down against an enemy army that was three times bigger than theirs. They didn't go down there with weapons. They also didn't go down there with their knees shaking — because God told them over and over again not to fear because the battle belonged to the Lord.

The Lord instructed Judah's singers to go down toward the enemy and fill the atmosphere with worship. The singers marched down to their enemy, saying over and over, "Praise the Lord, for His mercy endures forever," (2 Chronicles 20:21). Their focus was on who God is — not on one another or their enemy.

The people of Judah worshiped the Lord and magnified His name. As they told God who He is, the threat of the enemy became less and less. And look what happened when they reached their enemy's camp! Second Chronicles 20:22 says, "Now when they began to sing and to praise, the Lord set ambushes against the people of Ammon, Moab, and Mount Seir, who had come against Judah; and they were defeated." It was a *great* defeat!

The Spoils of the Battle Are Ours for the Taking

When you worship, who appears on the scene for you? The Lord! Just like He set ambushes against the enemies of Judah, the Lord will also fight on your behalf. The Scriptures tell us that the enemy soldiers turned on each other and destroyed each other. Then for three days the people of Israel collected the spoils — clothes, silver, and gold — everything of value that their enemy had.

This is what happens when we worship the Lord. He gives us the power and the peace to go and collect the spoils from our enemy, just as Denise's friend did. That mother sought the Lord when her daughter's life was threatened. God spoke to her and said, "Don't be afraid." And He intimidated the enemy. Through His Spirit, He came against that sickness and disease, and He healed that girl. And she's alive to this day.

Our praise and worship intimidates the enemy. It takes us to a place where we are not to be stolen from. Rather, we steal from the enemy and defeat his bad plans. We cancel them out in the powerful name of Jesus and the presence of God that is in us through worship. Heaven brings answers when we worship! Be encouraged today to open your heart to God, worship Him, and let Him bring you the answers you need.

STUDY QUESTIONS

Be diligent to present yourself approved to God, a worker
who does not need to be ashamed, rightly dividing the word of truth.
— 2 Timothy 2:15

1. In the midst of challenges, it is vital to hear, perceive, understand, and follow the leading of the Lord. Read John 10:27, John 16:13, and Romans 8:14. What does the Word say about following the leading of the Holy Spirit?
2. Read Philippians 2:9-11.
   What does it declare about the name of Jesus?
3. Read Jeremiah 29:13; Psalm 9:1; and Psalm 111:1.
   What does it mean to seek God wholeheartedly?

PRACTICAL APPLICATION

But be doers of the word,
and not hearers only, deceiving yourselves.
— James 1:22

1. As we learned in Second Chronicles 20:21, we should always make time to go before the Lord in song and praise, saying, "Praise the Lord, for His mercy endures forever." Take a moment now and allow God to reveal His goodness to you as you sing and praise Him for His never-ending mercy. Meditate on His mercy toward you and write out what He shows you along those lines.
2. That battle you're facing is not yours! It's the same for you today as it was for King Jehoshaphat. God is saying to you, "That's not your battle. You don't have to fight that battle. I've already fought it for you." Take time now to acknowledge that the battle you are facing is the Lord's, not yours. Let Him know you trust Him for the victory.
3. We saw in Second Chronicles 20:16 and 17 that in the midst of the battle, God gave instructions. God already knew where the enemy army was, so he told Jehoshaphat and the people of Judah where to go. The prophet of the Lord went on to explain what the people were to do. God may have instructions for you in the midst of the situation you are facing. Worship Him and listen for His leading and His direction. Write down what He says to you and obey Him. It may not

make sense to your mind, but if you follow His leading in your heart, all will be well.

TOPIC

You Are Strengthened Through Worship

SCRIPTURES

1. **1 Samuel 30:1-8** — Now it happened, when David and his men came to Ziklag, on the third day, that the Amalekites had invaded the South and Ziklag, attacked Ziklag and burned it with fire, and had taken captive the women and those who were there, from small to great; they did not kill anyone, but carried them away and went their way. So David and his men came to the city, and there it was, burned with fire; and their wives, their sons, and their daughters had been taken captive. Then David and the people who were with him lifted up their voices and wept, until they had no more power to weep. And David's two wives, Ahinoam the Jezreelitess, and Abigail the widow of Nabal the Carmelite, had been taken captive. Now David was greatly distressed, for the people spoke of stoning him, because the soul of all the people was grieved, every man for his sons and his daughters. But David strengthened himself in the Lord his God. Then David said to Abiathar the priest, Ahimelech's son, "Please bring the ephod here to me." And Abiathar brought the ephod to David. So David inquired of the Lord, saying, "Shall I pursue this troop? Shall I overtake them?" And He answered him, "Pursue, for you shall surely overtake them and without fail recover all."

2. **James 1:5** — If any of you lacks wisdom, let him ask of God, who gives to all liberally and without reproach, and it will be given to him.

3. **Romans 8:26** — Likewise the Spirit also helps in our weaknesses. For we do not know what we should pray for as we ought, but the Spirit Himself makes intercession for us with groanings which cannot be uttered.

4. **1 Corinthians 6:17** — But he who is joined to the Lord is one spirit with Him.

GREEK WORDS

1. "help" — συναντιλαμβάνομαι (*synantilambánomai*): to take hold with at the side, to take a share in, generally to help (*syn*): right alongside, (*anti*): ferociously against, (*lambánomai*): to take or to seize

SYNOPSIS

When an enemy army set fire to the city of Ziklag and kidnapped the women and children, King David's men were so distraught they wanted to stone him. But David strengthened himself in the Lord, prayed, and went in the power of God to recover all that had been stolen! And he recovered *all!* Today, the Holy Spirit dwells in us as our Helper who causes us to be victorious, just as David was. When we're faced with impossible situations, a key to victory is calling on God to help us.

The emphasis of this lesson:

No matter what we may face, we have the great Helper within us — the Holy Spirit! As we speak truth and worship God, the Holy Spirit arises to give us strength. He comes alongside us, stands ferociously against our enemy, and helps us take back what has been stolen from us. Through worship, we receive our victory!

Remember What the Lord Has Done

As the times we live in get more difficult and pressures and trials come upon us, we need to understand how powerful worship is. When we realize that worship opens Heaven with answers for us, our worship to God becomes deeper, and we come to understand more and more about who He is. And we can be strengthened in worship. We see this happening in First Samuel 30:1-6.

> **Now it happened, when David and his men came to Ziklag, on the third day, that the Amalekites had invaded the South and Ziklag, attacked Ziklag and burned it with fire, and had taken captive the women and those who were there, from small to great; they did not kill anyone, but carried them away and went their way. So David and his men came to the city, and there**

> it was, burned with fire; and their wives, their sons, and their
> daughters had been taken captive. Then David and the people
> who were with him lifted up their voices and wept, until they
> had no more power to weep. And David's two wives, Ahinoam
> the Jezreelitess, and Abigail the widow of Nabal the Carmelite,
> had been taken captive. Now David was greatly distressed,
> for the people spoke of stoning him, because the soul of all
> the people was grieved, every man for his sons and his daugh-
> ters. But David strengthened himself in the Lord his God.

When tragedy comes, we must strengthen ourselves in the Lord our God.
How do we do this? The Bible says many times that we are to remember
what the Lord did. When David was just a young boy, before he faced
Goliath, he recounted all the times God had brought him a victory.

David envisioned the giant falling down before him as he cut off his head.
He was just a young man, yet when he faced that huge giant, he essentially
said, "I know that you come to me with your sword and your spear, but I
come to you with the name of the Lord of hosts, and I will take you down
and I will feed your body to the birds" (*see* 1 Samuel 17:45-47). David had
that victory in his memory.

What do you have in your memory that God has already done for you?
Denise shared a memory from a time when she was recording an album.
Her voice wouldn't perform as it was supposed to, and she was frustrated.
She took a break and rehearsed everything that God had done in her life
to that point. She said, "After about fifteen minutes of rehearsing all the
things that God had done in my life, I went back in that studio, and I did
not have any more problems."

Strengthen Yourself in the Lord

When we remember what God has done for us, we stir up our faith and
strengthen ourselves. This is what David did after all the women and
children had been taken captive. But then he did something else. In First
Samuel 30:7, we read, "…David said to Abiathar the priest, Ahimelech's
son, 'Please bring the ephod here to me.' And Abiathar brought the ephod
to David." In response to a tragic situation, David did not fall into despair.
No, he strengthened himself in the Lord then asked for the ephod (which
represented prayer) and prayed.

As you can imagine, when the men returned to the city to find their homes and families gone, they held David responsible for what had happened and wanted to stone him. Their wives had been kidnapped, all of their sons and daughters had been taken, and their city had been burned to the ground — they lost everything. So in the face of all the animosity, it might have taken David some time to strengthen himself in the Lord.

Although it may also take us some time to strengthen ourselves in the Lord, we receive more and more strength as we continue to pray and read God's Word. We become less downcast and more encouraged. We can go to God in prayer and tell Him what we need and pour our hearts out to him regarding the situation. But it is important to position ourselves in that place of worship and prayer to the Lord and say things like, "You are God. You can handle this, and I trust You."

Instead of being overcome by the problem, strengthen yourself in the Lord by remembering all He has done for you in the past. Maybe He healed your body or delivered you out of a financial mess that was impossible to solve on your own. Maybe He saved your child or touched your husband's heart. Maybe He brought peace to a relationship that seemed too far gone for restoration. Remember the things He has done for you!

First Samuel 30:8 says, "So David inquired of the Lord, saying, 'Shall I pursue this troop? Shall I overtake them?' And He answered him, 'Pursue, for you shall surely overtake them and without fail recover all.'" And David went into the enemy's camp and defeated them.

David and his men got all their wives and children back. Not only did they recover all that had been stolen from them, but they got the spoils of the enemy as well. Because David responded with worship and prayer, he positioned himself to receive answers for how to handle the troubling situation and take back what rightfully belonged to him — *and more*! This is the power of worship!

God Gives His Wisdom Liberally

To receive answers from Heaven for our own lives, we can follow David's example. First, we strengthen ourselves in the Lord by remembering what He has done for us. Second, we ask Him and make our petition. Third, we inquire of Him for guidance.

You see, prayer is not religious. Prayer is a conversation with Almighty God; it is communion with Him. When we come to Him, we must expect His answers. He says, "Call to Me, and I will answer you…" (Jeremiah 33:3). The Bible says in James 1:5, "If any of you lacks wisdom, let him ask of God, who gives to all liberally and without reproach, and it will be given to him." If we need wisdom, we're to ask Him, and He'll give it to us liberally. God is not trying to hold back answers *from* us. He's trying to get the answers *to* us. And when we open our heart and worship Him, we can hear God speaking to us.

When troubling circumstances arise, we often find ourselves in desperate need for help that is beyond us. But something very powerful happens when we worship God in response to or in the midst of a difficult or even tragic situation. Romans 8:26 says, "Likewise the Spirit also helps in our weaknesses. For we do not know what we should pray for as we ought, but the Spirit Himself makes intercession for us with groanings which cannot be uttered."

Have you ever been in a situation where you didn't know how to pray, and it didn't seem like your prayers were very powerful? In those times, the Holy Spirit is there to help you. When you worship God, you acknowledge who He is. You recognize Him as your Helper and Deliverer. You align yourself with the One who has the answers when you say, "Holy Spirit, help me."

The Holy Spirit Is Present To Help You

In the Greek language, the word "help" is *synantilambánomai*. The first part of this word, *syn*, means *alongside*. When we say, "Help me, Holy Spirit," immediately, He is alongside us with His companionship and fellowship. First Corinthians 6:17 says, "But he who is joined to the Lord is one spirit with Him." We are one with the Holy Spirit, so when we worship and acknowledge Him, we open ourselves up to what the Holy Spirit wants to do. As soon as we call out for help, He comes right alongside us.

The second part of that word is *anti*. The word *anti* does not just mean, "I am against you." *Anti* means *ferociously against*. When the enemy comes and tries to take us down or tell us lies, the Holy Spirit on the inside of us is ready to defeat him! He's so angry that He's ready to take the enemy and throw him down. That's what the word *anti* means. We have such a friend in the Holy Spirit! He's *syn,* meaning *alongside* us. And He's such a fighter! He's *anti,* depicting that He is *ferociously against* our enemy.

This very Holy Spirit is in you right now! No matter what you're facing, when you ask Him to help, He is right *alongside* you (*syn*). He is totally, *ferociously against* (*anti*) the thing that's against you, and He wants to take hold of it and throw it down.

The last part of the word "help" is *lambánomai,* meaning *to take or to seize.* Imagine you are walking down the street with your purse on your arm or wallet in your hand, and someone takes your purse from you. That thief has grabbed it and made it his own. That's what the Holy Spirit does when we ask for help. He comes alongside us, and His attitude is ferocious to take our enemy down. With His power, He grabs hold of that enemy or that lie, and He makes it His own, giving you the victory.

Align Yourself With the Helper Inside You

David strengthened himself in the Lord, and we can too. He prayed to the Lord, and we can as well. He inquired of the Lord, and so can we because we have on the inside of us the magnificent, powerful Helper. The Holy Spirit who dwells within us wants to come into our situation as we worship the Lord and align ourselves with Him.

When you worship the Lord, you align yourself with His power. You choose to line up with Him, instead of siding with the negative thoughts or feelings that tell you you'll never be delivered from your troubling situation. No! When the onslaught of those thoughts come and the enemy is speaking, remember this: *You are not alone.*

David wasn't alone either. At that time, God had not yet taken up residence on the inside of man, so David did not have the Holy Spirit inside him. But the Holy Spirit — the Helper, the Comforter, the Teacher — is on the inside of *you!* He's ready to help you, and worship opens the door for you to hear answers from Heaven through Him.

Do you need to hear answers from Heaven? Worship the Lord. Get quiet and read the Psalms to Him. Say things like, "Lord, You are magnificent. You know the situation that I'm in, but I declare You as my Savior and my Lord. You are coming again, and You will take us up into Heaven with You so we can spend eternity with You. When You forgave me of my sins,

You blotted them out and separated my sins from me as far as the east is from the west."

Speak the truth about who you are and who He is, saying things like, "Lord, I thank You that because of Jesus who knew no sin, I became the righteousness of God in Him. I thank You that by the stripes of Jesus, I was healed." Worship the Lord for who He is: our Lord, our great High Priest, the Everlasting Father, the Prince of Peace, the soon-coming King, the Great Shepherd, the I AM, the First and the Last!

Worship Invites Him Into Your Circumstances

When we worship Him, His presence comes. So regardless of what you may need, worshiping Him is *always* appropriate. There is no situation too bad or too dire for you to raise your hands and worship Him — despite how you may feel or what is going on around you. You can always worship Him as your God and your Savior. The salvation that Jesus purchased for you on the Cross is enough for you today and carries the delivering and saving power that you need. His amazing Holy Spirit that He put inside you is just like Jesus, and He will never change. He is the same yesterday, today, and forever (*see* Hebrews 13:8).

When you speak the truth and worship Him, His presence comes. And when His presence comes, joy, peace, and healing come. Answers come because He loves you so much and doesn't want to hold back anything from you. Romans 8:32 says, "He who did not spare His own Son, but delivered Him up for us all, how shall He not with Him also freely give us all things?"

When you worship the Lord and line yourself up with Him, telling Him who He is and who you are in Him, you strengthen yourself so that you can say, in faith, "Holy Spirit, help me." When you call out to God, He comes rushing in with answers because that's who He is — your Helper. He's exactly what you need. When you call out to God, He responds with His fellowship and closeness. He is always for you and on your side. He's against the enemy, and He's going to take him down. Declare this over yourself right now:

Thank You, Lord, for the power of Your presence. Right now, I call out to You, Holy Spirit — help me. I receive Your answers. I receive Your fellowship. I receive Your power to take down my enemy, in Jesus' name, amen.

STUDY QUESTIONS

Be diligent to present yourself approved to God, a worker
who does not need to be ashamed, rightly dividing the word of truth.
— 2 Timothy 2:15

1. Read John 14:16, John 14:26, and John 15:26. What does God's Word teach us about one of the Holy Spirit's main roles in the life of a believer?

2. David prayed when he needed guidance on what to do. What does the Bible teach us about asking God for direction? Read Jeremiah 33:3; Psalm 18:3; Psalm 34:6; and Psalm 50:15.

3. Read First Corinthians 3:16 and First Corinthians 6:19 and 20. What does the Word of God tell us about the Holy Spirit's dwelling place?

PRACTICAL APPLICATION

But be doers of the word,
and not hearers only, deceiving yourselves.
— James 1:22

1. When trouble came, David strengthened himself in the Lord his God. Are you facing challenging circumstances? Take time now to strengthen yourself in the Lord your God. There's no need to wait for someone else to encourage you. Receive strength by praising God with your whole heart now. Notice how when you lift up your voice and magnify Him, He infuses you with His strength.

2. In the program, we learned that when we remember what God has done for us, we stir up our own faith and strengthen ourselves. Remember what the Lord has done in your life. Recall His faithfulness. Realize how He helped you in the past and He will help you now in the situation you are facing — as you worship Him. Make a list of what the Lord has done for you and take a few moments to praise Him for those things!

3. When the wives, sons, and daughters of Ziklag were taken captive and the enemy burned the city to the ground, David and his men were greatly distressed. David was not only facing the distress of losing his family and home, but he was also facing the accusations of his men and carrying the burden of responsibility for what had happened. But

David inquired of the Lord about what to do. Is something distressing you? Inquire of the Lord! Write down any direction He gives you and obey His leading in the situation.

TOPIC

Worship Can Shake Things Up

SCRIPTURES

1. **Acts 16:16-19** — Now it happened, as we went to prayer, that a certain slave girl possessed with a spirit of divination met us, who brought her masters much profit by fortune-telling. This girl followed Paul and us, and cried out, saying, "These men are the servants of the Most High God, who proclaim to us the way of salvation." And this she did for many days. But Paul, greatly annoyed, turned and said to the spirit, "I command you in the name of Jesus Christ to come out of her." And he came out that very hour. But when her masters saw that their hope of profit was gone, they seized Paul and Silas and dragged them into the marketplace to the authorities.

2. **Acts 16:20-34** — And they brought them to the magistrates, and said, "These men, being Jews, exceedingly trouble our city; and they teach customs which are not lawful for us, being Romans, to receive or observe." Then the multitude rose up together against them; and the magistrates tore off their clothes and commanded them to be beaten with rods. And when they had laid many stripes on them, they threw them into prison, commanding the jailer to keep them securely. Having received such a charge, he put them into the inner prison and fastened their feet in the stocks. But at midnight Paul and Silas were praying and singing hymns to God, and the prisoners were listening to them. Suddenly there was a great earthquake, so that the foundations of the prison were shaken; and immediately all the doors were opened and everyone's chains were loosed. And the keeper of the prison, awaking from sleep and seeing the prison doors open, supposing the prisoners had fled, drew his sword and was about to kill himself. But Paul called with a loud voice, saying, "Do yourself no harm, for we are all here." Then he called for a light, ran in, and

fell down trembling before Paul and Silas. And he brought them out and said, "Sirs, what must I do to be saved?" So they said, "Believe on the Lord Jesus Christ, and you will be saved, you and your household." Then they spoke the word of the Lord to him and to all who were in his house. And he took them the same hour of the night and washed their stripes. And immediately he and all his family were baptized. Now when he had brought them into his house, he set food before them; and he rejoiced, having believed in God with all his household.

3. **2 Timothy 2:11-13** — This is a faithful saying: For if we died with Him, we shall also live with Him. If we endure, we shall also reign with Him. If we deny Him, He also will deny us. If we are faithless, He remains faithful; He cannot deny Himself.

4. **Psalm 149:5-9** — Let the saints be joyful in glory; let them sing aloud on their beds. Let the high praises of God be in their mouth, and a two-edged sword in their hand, to execute vengeance on the nations, and punishments on the peoples; to bind their kings with chains, and their nobles with fetters of iron; to execute on them the written judgment — this honor have all His saints. Praise the Lord!

5. **1 Corinthians 15:55** — "O Death, where is your sting? O Hades, where is your victory?"

6. **Romans 8:37-39** — Yet in all these things we are more than conquerors through Him who loved us. For I am persuaded that neither death nor life, nor angels nor principalities nor powers, nor things present nor things to come, nor height nor depth, nor any other created thing, shall be able to separate us from the love of God which is in Christ Jesus our Lord.

SYNOPSIS

Our worship brings God's power into our circumstances. This is clearly seen in Acts 16. A young woman possessed by a spirit of divination harassed Paul and Silas as they ministered the Gospel. Paul cast the demon out, and as a result, he and Silas were tortured and thrown into prison. In the midnight hour, they sang praises to God, and a mighty earthquake freed them from their chains! They shared the Gospel with the jailer, and he and his entire household were saved. Through our praises, we can access the same divine power to see *our* circumstances mightily changed!

The emphasis of this lesson:

When we worship, we receive answers from Heaven. When we ask of God, He liberally gives us wisdom to help us (*see* James 1:5). As we worship God, we're aligning ourselves with His will and with Him. And when we're aligned with Him, it's much easier to receive His answers.

Worship is so powerful that it shakes things up. It brings things into order. In Acts 16:16 and 17, a young demon-possessed girl kept coming around Paul and Silas. For many days, she would follow them and cry out, saying, "These men are the servants of the Most High God, who proclaim to us the way of salvation."

Eventually, Paul became grieved because in his heart, he understood that she was not speaking by the Spirit of God, but she was speaking by a demonic spirit. Acts 16:18 and 19 says:

> **…But Paul, greatly annoyed, turned and said to the spirit, 'I command you in the name of Jesus Christ to come out of her.' And he came out that very hour. But when her masters saw that their hope of profit was gone, they seized Paul and Silas and dragged them into the marketplace to the authorities.**

When this young girl got delivered, she was no longer useful to her masters, because she could no longer bring them profit. As a result, they grew upset. Acts 16:20-22 says, "And they brought them to the magistrates, and said, 'These men, being Jews, exceedingly trouble our city; and they teach customs which are not lawful for us, being Romans, to receive or observe.' Then the multitude rose up together against them; and the magistrates tore off their clothes and commanded them to be beaten with rods."

Paul and Silas Endured Torture

The crowd became upset and wanted to punish the ones who caused the riot — and they blamed Paul and Silas. Acts 16:23 and 24 says,

> **And when they had laid many stripes on them, they threw them into prison, commanding the jailer to keep them securely. Having received such a charge, he put them into the inner prison and fastened their feet in the stocks.**

According to Acts 16:24, Paul and Silas were put in the "inner prison" — the dungeon. The authorities fastened Paul's and Silas's feet in stocks, which was torture. Their legs were spread apart, and iron was placed around their legs and locked to the wall. Imagine how painful that must have been. Not to mention the fact that they had been beaten before they were placed in prison.

Acts 16:25 says, "But at midnight Paul and Silas were praying and singing hymns to God, and the prisoners were listening to them." They were beaten and then imprisoned in painful stocks for 12 hours. Yet at midnight they began to sing and praise God.

Chained in that inner prison, Paul and Silas sang so loudly that other prisoners heard them. We don't know which song they sang, but historians say that the verses in Second Timothy 2:11-13 were a song they might have sung: "For if we died with Him, we shall also live with Him. If we endure, we shall also reign with Him. If we deny Him, He also will deny us. If we are faithless, He remains faithful; He cannot deny Himself." Can you imagine them singing so loudly in faith?

We Were Created To Sing His Praises

When the enemy comes against you, start singing! Praise God with a song. You can sing things like: "I worship You, Lord. You are my God. There is no other like You, Father." Sing a song that you learned at church or make up your own — it doesn't matter. Just start singing!

Did you know that of all the other creatures on the planet, none of them is a speaking spirit, and none of them can sing a song of worship from his or her heart? When children begin to speak, even that, in itself, is a miracle of creation. It's a miracle of God's design that babies can speak and imitate their parents. But to sing? We are made in God's image, and we were especially created to sing His praises.

God knows your voice, and when you lift your voice to Him, He recognizes that it's you. He hears you singing, and your worship is like a sweet aroma unto Him. It doesn't matter if you don't have a pretty voice. When He hears your voice and your praise, it comes up before Him like a fragrance. When you sing, you are like no other person. Sing to God, and it will bring His presence right into your situation as you worship Him.

God Responds to Our Worship
With His Deliverance

We know the end of Paul and Silas' story, but at the time, they didn't know what would happen to them. They were in the inner prison with their legs in stocks, beaten, bleeding, and in pain as they sang to God.

Acts 16:26 says, "Suddenly there was a great earthquake, so that the foundations of the prison were shaken; and immediately all the doors were opened and everyone's chains were loosed." An earthquake supernaturally came to those jail cells and freed those prisoners from their stocks!

God's power is so mighty! When we start praising Him, He comes with his power to loose us from our bonds. And what happened next was awesome. Acts 16:27 and 28 says, "And the keeper of the prison, awaking from sleep and seeing the prison doors open, supposing the prisoners had fled, drew his sword and was about to kill himself. But Paul called with a loud voice, saying, 'Do yourself no harm, for we are all here.'"

The jailer knew that he would die if the prisoners got loose, so he was ready to pierce himself with his sword and commit suicide. Paul and Silas said, "Don't do that! We're here." Acts 16:29-31 says, "Then he called for a light, ran in, and fell down trembling before Paul and Silas. And he brought them out and said, 'Sirs, what must I do to be saved?' So they said, 'Believe on the Lord Jesus Christ, and you will be saved, you and your household.'"

The jailer was so grateful that he took Paul and Silas home with him and treated their wounds. Paul and Silas preached, and the jailer's whole household was saved. The door to that powerful miracle was opened by praise and worship!

We Have the Victory in Christ Jesus

The Bible gives us a picture of what God will do on our behalf against evil principalities and powers when we praise and worship Him. When the Word of God is in our song of worship and praise, the evil rulers of darkness of this world don't stand a chance, and we can pull down those strongholds in our minds that try to overcome us.

Psalm 149:5 and 6 says, "Let the saints be joyful in glory; let them sing aloud on their beds. Let the high praises of God be in their mouth, and a two-edged sword in their hand…." When we sing God's Word, it comes out of our mouth like a sword to pierce right in the middle of the enemy's plan.

Psalm 149:7 declares further, "To execute vengeance on the nations, and punishments on the peoples." When the enemy tries to come against you, you can bring punishment on him with your praise. Verse 8 says, "To bind their kings with chains…." Remember, Paul and Silas were in chains, but when they started praising and singing to God, an earthquake came and loosed their chains.

When you are in the midst of a bad situation, you can decide to praise the Lord. Regardless of what is going on, He is still God, and you can choose to praise Him in the midst of it all. You can stand firm with the knowledge of who He is and who you are in Him. You can "execute vengeance" on your enemy through your praise.

Verses 8 and 9 of Psalm 149 go on to say, "To bind their kings with chains, and their nobles with fetters of iron; to execute on them the written judgment — this honor have all His saints. Praise the Lord!" When we agree with God, we are executing the judgment that has already been written.

First Corinthians 15:55 says, "O Death, where is your sting? O Hades, where is your victory?" Jesus swallowed up death and hell and the grave with His victory on the Cross. He took from us that old sinful nature and gave to us a brand-new nature (*see* 2 Corinthians 5:17).

It is written that we are victors in Christ Jesus (*see* 1 Corinthians 15:57). The Bible says we're more than overcomers through Christ Jesus who loved us (*see* Romans 8:37). When we agree with what's written about our God and what's written about us, we execute vengeance on our enemy. When we say, "By the stripes of Jesus, I am healed," we are declaring what is written (*see* 1 Peter 2:24). When we say, "I am the righteousness of God in Christ. Jesus was made sin who knew no sin, that I might be the righteousness of God in Him," we are saying what is written (*see* 2 Corinthians 5:21), and we are executing vengeance and judgment on the enemy.

This is so glorious. If the enemy is jeering and trying to intimidate you, execute judgment on him by speaking what is written. Agree with God — not your feelings, not the enemy, and not your thoughts. Pull down those thoughts, exercising your authority by acknowledging what is written in God's Word.

We Are More Than Conquerors Through Him Who Loved Us

Our salvation is magnificent! We are such overcomers that it says in Romans 8:37, "Yet in *all these things* we are more than conquerors through Him who loved us." What things was Paul talking about? He was referring to the things that come against us. We are more than conquerors through Christ over all the things that come against us in life.

Romans 8:38 and 39 says, "For I am persuaded that neither death nor life, nor angels nor principalities nor powers, nor things present nor things to come, nor height nor depth, nor any other created thing, shall be able to separate us from the love of God which is in Christ Jesus our Lord."

In these verses, Paul wasn't just talking about himself in this verse. He said, "…[nothing] shall be able to separate *us*…" That little word "us" includes you! Therefore, you can boldly and confidently say, "Nothing shall be able to separate *me* from the love of God which is in Christ Jesus *my* Lord."

Declaring the Word of God and standing by what is written is in itself a judgment on the enemy. He knows his time is short. He knows he is going to be in hell forever because he knows the judgment that has already been written — he knows his sentence.

Ultimately, the only thing the enemy can bring against us is deception. If we believe his lies, we'll be deceived. But if we stand and praise our God and agree with the judgment that has been written, it will bring vengeance upon him. That's the power God has given us.

Resurrection Power Lives Within Us

The very resurrection power of Christ — the power that raised Jesus from the dead — lives on the inside of us, and the way we exercise that power is with our voice. The Bible says, "Therefore submit to God. Resist the devil and he will flee from you" (James 4:7). By declaring the Word of God, we activate the power of God within us to resist the enemy.

When the enemy comes, he comes with so much fury. But we have magnificent power through praise and worship to shake things up and execute the Word of God on our enemy and stop him right in the middle of his attack. Through our worship and praise, we have access to the same power that raised Christ from the grave and to every answer we need.

STUDY QUESTIONS

*Be diligent to present yourself approved to God, a worker
who does not need to be ashamed, rightly dividing the word of truth.*
— 2 Timothy 2:15

1. When we praise God, one of the things He does is respond with His power to loose us from our bands. Read Psalm 8:2; Psalm 18:3; and Psalm 27:4 and 5. What else does God's Word teach us about what happens when we praise Him?

2. Praise is a choice. It is an act of our will — particularly when we're in the midst of facing the challenging storms of life. Psalm 16:7 says, "I *will* bless the Lord...." Do you have to feel like praising God in order to praise Him? Why is it important to praise Him even when your flesh doesn't feel like it?

3. Read Genesis 1:26 and 27 and Psalm 139:14. You are made in the image of God! When you sing to Him, He knows your voice. What else does the Bible say about the way God made you?

PRACTICAL APPLICATION

*But be doers of the word,
and not hearers only, deceiving yourselves.*
— James 1:22

1. When the enemy came against Paul and Silas, they found themselves in the inner prison. But in the midst of that challenging circumstance, they prayed and sang praises to God. Take time now to pray and sing praises to the Lord in the midst of the problems you are facing. When you do, the presence of God will inhabit your praises and bring answers. Glory to God!

2. We're to exercise our authority by declaring what is written. What is written in the Word about you? Take time to declare God's Word now by faith:

   • "...Thanks be to God, who gives us the victory through our Lord Jesus Christ" (1 Corinthians 15:57).

   • "...In all these things we are more than conquerors through Him who loved us" (Romans 8:37).

- "Now thanks be to God who always leads us in triumph in Christ, and through us diffuses the fragrance of His knowledge in every place" (2 Corinthians 2:14).

3. When thoughts come that are not in line with God's Word, we are to cast them down. "Casting down arguments and every high thing that exalts itself against the knowledge of God, bringing every thought into captivity to the obedience of Christ" (2 Corinthians 10:5). Take a few minutes to cast down any thoughts you have had that don't line up with God's Word. Replace those thoughts with what Philippians 4:8 (*KJV*) instructs: "Finally, brethren, whatever things are true, whatever things are noble, whatever things are just, whatever things are pure, whatever things are lovely, whatever things are of good report, if there is any virtue and if there is anything praiseworthy — meditate on these things.

LESSON 5

TOPIC

Ultimate Worship

SCRIPTURES

1. **Revelation 4:8-11** — The four living creatures, each having six wings, were full of eyes around and within. And they do not rest day or night, saying: "Holy, holy, holy, Lord God Almighty, Who was and is and is to come!" Whenever the living creatures give glory and honor and thanks to Him who sits on the throne, who lives forever and ever, the twenty-four elders fall down before Him who sits on the throne and worship Him who lives forever and ever, and cast their crowns before the throne, saying: "You are worthy, O Lord, to receive glory and honor and power; for You created all things, and by Your will they exist and were created."

2. **Revelation 5:9-14** — And they sang a new song, saying: "You are worthy to take the scroll, and to open its seals; for You were slain, and have redeemed us to God by Your blood out of every tribe and tongue and people and nation, and have made us kings and priests to our God; and we shall reign on the earth." Then I looked, and I heard the

voice of many angels around the throne, the living creatures, and the elders; and the number of them was ten thousand times ten thousand, and thousands of thousands, saying with a loud voice: "Worthy is the Lamb who was slain to receive power and riches and wisdom, and strength and honor and glory and blessing!" And every creature which is in heaven and on the earth and under the earth and such as are in the sea, and all that are in them, I heard saying: "Blessing and honor and glory and power be to Him who sits on the throne, and to the Lamb, forever and ever!" Then the four living creatures said, "Amen!" And the twenty-four elders fell down and worshiped Him who lives forever and ever.

3. **Philippians 2:9-11** — Therefore God also has highly exalted Him and given Him the name which is above every name, that at the name of Jesus every knee should bow, of those in heaven, and of those on earth, and of those under the earth, and that every tongue should confess that Jesus Christ is Lord, to the glory of God the Father.

4. **Matthew 11:28-30** — Come to Me, all you who labor and are heavy laden, and I will give you rest. Take My yoke upon you and learn from Me, for I am gentle and lowly in heart, and you will find rest for your souls. For My yoke is easy and My burden is light.

5. **1 Peter 5:7** — Casting all your care upon Him, for He cares for you.

SYNOPSIS

Revelation 4 and 5 show us the culmination of our relationship with God — the ultimate worship found in Heaven. All the saints will be gathered together, singing glory to God before His throne forever. He is the God who answers when we call upon Him in faith. He has performed miracles for His people throughout the ages. The very same God who is worshiped in Heaven lives within us, and His miracle-working power is present with us even now as we praise Him! And there is coming a day when all creatures — those in Heaven, on earth, and under the earth, saints and sinners alike — will bow their knee and declare that Jesus is Lord.

The emphasis of this lesson:

It is our destiny — both now and forevermore — to worship the Lord and give Him glory. This same God who awaits our arrival in Heaven has been present for His saints throughout the ages, doing miracles and showing up to deliver and to save. And He is with us right now to do the

same. Through worship, the power of God comes into our lives to cause anything that is coming against us to bow to His mighty name!

Heaven opens when we worship! And when we need answers, our Heavenly Father wants to give them to us. Answers come to us when we quiet ourselves before God and give Him our full attention and spend time in His presence. When we do this, we find everything we need.

The Ultimate Example of Worship

What does true worship look like? What is the *ultimate* example of worship? We will eventually spend eternity worshiping God in Heaven, so it would be good to find out what that will be like! We have an amazing picture of it in Revelation 4:8-11, which says:

> The four living creatures, each having six wings, were full of eyes around and within. And they do not rest day or night, saying: 'Holy, holy, holy, Lord God Almighty, Who was and is and is to come!' Whenever the living creatures give glory and honor and thanks to Him who sits on the throne, who lives forever and ever, the twenty-four elders fall down before Him who sits on the throne and worship Him who lives forever and ever, and cast their crowns before the throne, saying: 'You are worthy, O Lord, to receive glory and honor and power; for You created all things, and by Your will they exist and were created.'

What a beautiful example of worship. This is what's going on right now in Heaven; they are continually crying, "You are worthy, O Lord!" According to Revelation 5:9-14, this kind of worship goes on and on. The Lord is receiving this kind of worship non-stop!

> And they sang a new song, saying: 'You are worthy to take the scroll, and to open its seals; for You were slain, and have redeemed us to God by Your blood out of every tribe and tongue and people and nation, and have made us kings and priests to our God; and we shall reign on the earth.' Then I looked, and I heard the voice of many angels around the throne, the living creatures, and the elders; and the number of them was ten thousand times ten thousand, and thousands of thousands, saying with a loud voice: 'Worthy is the Lamb who was slain to receive power and riches and wisdom, and strength and honor and glory and blessing!'

And every creature which is in heaven and on the earth and under the earth and such as are in the sea, and all that are in them, I heard saying: 'Blessing and honor and glory and power be to Him who sits on the throne, and to the Lamb, forever and ever!' Then the four living creatures said, 'Amen!' And the twenty-four elders fell down and worshiped Him who lives forever and ever.

Every creature on the earth will declare that He is worthy! All of creation is going to praise Him. All of creation will declare that all blessing, honor, glory, and power belongs to Him.

The Same God Lives in Us

The God who is worshiped in Revelation is our very same God, Savior, and best friend. The God who appeared in the Old and New Testaments is the same God who lives in us.

He is the God who:

- Sticks closer than a brother (Proverbs 18:24).
- Lives on the inside of us (Galatians 2:20).
- Stopped the lion's mouth when Daniel was in the den of the lions (Daniel 6:10-23).
- Appeared to Hagar when she was running for her life from Sarah (Genesis 16).
- Walked in the midst of the fiery furnace with Shadrach, Meshach, and Abednego (Daniel 3:19-25).
- Split the Red Sea (Exodus 14).
- Fed the Israelites manna every day from Heaven (Exodus 16).
- Wrestled with Jacob and changed his name (Genesis 32:22-32).
- Sent an angel and defeated 185,000 Assyrians (2 Kings 19:35).
- Caused Elisha's bones to raise someone from the dead (2 Kings 13:21).
- Was born of a virgin (Matthew 1:18-23).
- Turned the water into wine (John 2:1-12).
- Fed the 5,000 (Matthew 14:13-21).
- Opened blind Bartimaeus's eyes (Mark 10:46-52).

- Raised Lazarus from the dead (John 11:1-44).
- Healed the lepers (Luke 17:11-19).
- Raised from the dead the only son of a widow woman (Luke 7:11-17).
- Endured the whipping post, was denied by his friends, and hung on the Cross naked (John 19; Luke 22:54-62).
- Spoke to the thief on the cross and opened paradise up to him (Luke 23:39-43).
- Cried out from the Cross and said, "Father, forgive them, for they do not know what they do" (Luke 23:34).
- Rose from the dead and now is seated at the right hand of the Father (1 Peter 3:21,22).
- Poured out His own blood for us (Luke 22:20).
- Intercedes for us (Romans 8:34).

He is the God we will worship forever. He is the one who saved us, forgave us, caused us to be the righteousness of God in Christ Jesus, and put His very self on the inside of us. He is a holy, mighty God who works incredible miracles and deserves every ounce of worship that could ever be expressed. This is our God — *and He lives in us!*

Every Knee Will Bow

The ultimate worship we see in Revelation is our future. Someday *we* will be the ones saying, "Blessing and honor and glory and power be unto Him who sits on the throne and unto the Lamb forever and ever!" Our worship here on Earth is very powerful because it is a precursor to the worship we will be giving to Him when we get to Heaven.

God placed a deposit of Heaven on the inside of us, and from that place, we can worship Him. It's just a speck of what will be in front of us when we see Him with our own eyes. The worship we're practicing down here, this very worship that can come out of our heart and mouth right now, is going to continue forever and ever.

There will be a moment when every creature on the earth and in the sea will worship Him. There is coming a day when even the most evil of people will be on their knees, and they will say out of their mouths that Jesus Christ is Lord to the glory of God the Father. Philippians 2:9 and 11 says:

Therefore God also has highly exalted Him and given Him the name which is above every name, that at the name of Jesus every knee should bow, of those in heaven, and of those on earth, and of those under the earth, and that every tongue should confess that Jesus Christ is Lord, to the glory of God the Father.

One day, all of creation — everything in Heaven, on the earth, and under the earth — will worship Him. Every man, woman, boy, and girl who ever lived will be on their knees declaring, "Jesus is Lord to the glory of God the Father."

His Yoke Is Easy, and His Burden Is Light

As we live our life in the here and now, we have the opportunity to truly worship Him. And the beautiful thing about it is that through our worship, we bring Him right into our situation — even when it feels like our life is being turned upside down and we don't know which way to turn.

When we worship Him this way, we invite Heaven's presence right there with us. When we open our mouth and give God praise, we stir up the wonderful Holy Spirit who is inside us, called to be alongside us, and is angry at our enemy and ready to take him down.

God loves us so much! He doesn't hold back answers from us. He's not the God with the clenched fist. He's the God with the open hand. Jesus said in Matthew 11:28-30, "Come to Me, all you who labor and are heavy laden, and I will give you rest. Take My yoke upon you and learn from Me, for I am gentle and lowly in heart, and you will find rest for your souls. For My yoke is easy and My burden is light."

You may be carrying a burden, but it's time to give it over to the Lord. First Peter 5:7 says, "Casting all your care upon Him, for He cares for you." He's right there for you to unload your burdens on Him. He's the only one who can carry it. He did not make your shoulders to carry those burdens or the worries of those who are around you. Cast your cares and burdens over onto His shoulders and exchange it for His light burden.

When we worship Him, His presence comes. And with His presence comes everything good and everything we could ever need. His peace, joy, patience, long-suffering, understanding, kindness, and miracle-working power are all found in His presence when we worship Him.

STUDY QUESTIONS

**Be diligent to present yourself approved to God, a worker
who does not need to be ashamed, rightly dividing the word of truth.
— 2 Timothy 2:15**

1. Isaiah 26:3 says, "You will keep him in perfect peace, whose mind is stayed on You, because he trusts in You." When we quiet ourselves and set our hearts on God, He floods us with His peace. Read Second Corinthians 13:11, Philippians 4:6 and 7, and Colossians 3:15. What else does God's Word tell us we can do to receive and walk in His peace?

2. In this lesson, we learned about casting our cares on the Lord (*see* First Peter 5:7). Read Matthew 11:28-30. Where should we go when we are burdened?

3. God placed a deposit of Heaven on the inside of us, and from that place we can worship Him. Read John 4:24 and Psalm 29:2. What does the Bible teach us about worshiping God?

PRACTICAL APPLICATION

**But be doers of the word,
and not hearers only, deceiving yourselves.
— James 1:22**

1. Hebrews 4:9 says, "There remains therefore a rest for the people of God." You may be carrying a burden, but your shoulders were not made to carry heavy burdens, so cast them onto the Lord and enter into His rest.

2. The ultimate worship we see in the book of Revelation is our future. Take time right now to worship the Lord from your heart. Let Him know how wonderful He is to you and praise His name. It is in the place of worship — in the presence of God — that we find answers for everything we could ever need.

A Prayer To Receive Salvation

If you've never received Jesus as your Savior and Lord, now is the time for you to experience the new life Jesus wants to give you! To receive God's gift of salvation that can be obtained through Jesus alone, pray this prayer from your heart:

Jesus, I repent of my sin and receive You as my Savior and Lord. Wash away my sin with Your precious blood and make me completely new. I thank You that my sin is removed, and Satan no longer has any right to lay claim on me. Through Your empowering grace, I faithfully promise that I will serve You as my Lord for the rest of my life.

If you just prayed this prayer of salvation, you are born again! You are a brand-new creation in Christ! Would you please let us know of your decision by going to **renner.org/salvation**? We would love to connect with you and pray for you as you begin your new life in Christ.

Scriptures for further study: John 3:16; John 14:6; Acts 4:12; Ephesians 1:7; Hebrews 10:19,20; 1 Peter 1:18,19; Romans 10:9,10; Colossians 1:13; 2 Corinthians 5:17; Romans 6:4; 1 Peter 1:3

CLAIM YOUR FREE RESOURCE!

As a way of introducing you further to the teaching ministry of Rick Renner, we would like to send you FREE of charge his teaching, "How To Receive a Miraculous Touch From God" on CD or as an MP3 download.

In His earthly ministry, Jesus commonly healed *all* who were sick of *all* their diseases. In this profound message, learn about the manifold dimensions of Christ's wisdom, goodness, power, and love toward all humanity who came to Him in faith with their needs.

☑ **YES, I want to receive Rick Renner's monthly teaching letter!**

Simply scan the QR code to claim this resource or go to: **renner.org/claim-your-free-offer**

Connect
WITH US!

🏠 renner.org

f facebook.com/rickrenner • facebook.com/rennerdenise

▶ youtube.com/rennerministries • youtube.com/deniserenner

📷 instagram.com/rickrrenner • instagram.com/rennerministries_
instagram.com/rennerdenise